COUNTRY PROFILE: ALGERIA

COUNTRY

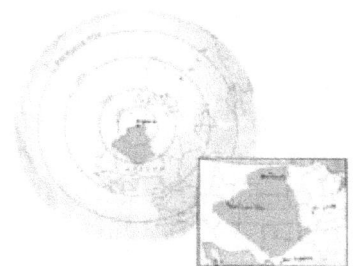

Formal Name: People's Democratic Republic of Algeria (Al Jumhuriyah al Jazairiyah ad Dimuqratiyah ash Shabiyah).

Short Form: Algeria (Al Jazair).

Term for Citizen(s): Algerian(s).

Click to Enlarge Image

Capital: Algiers, with a population of about 1.7 million, or 3 million including suburbs, in 2004.

Major Cities: After Algiers, the most populous cities are Oran, Constantine, and Annaba. According to 2004 estimates, Oran has a population of 700,000; Constantine, 350,000; and Annaba, 235,000.

Independence: Algeria celebrates independence from France on July 5, 1962.

Public Holidays: Official holidays include New Year's (January 1); Ashoura (January 19, 2008*); Birth of Muhammad (March 20, 2008*); Labor Day (May 1); Ben Bella's Overthrow (June 19); Independence Day (July 5); Ascension of Muhammad (July 30, 2008*); Beginning of Ramadan (September 1, 2008*); End of Ramadan (October 1, 2008*); Anniversary of the Revolution (November 1); Feast of the Sacrifice (December 8, 2008*); and Islamic New Year (December 29, 2008*). Dates marked with an asterisk vary from year to year according to the Islamic calendar.

Flag: Algeria's flag features a red crescent and a red five-pointed star against two equal vertical bands of green and white in the background. The crescent, the star, and the color green symbolize Islam, the state religion.

Click to Enlarge Image

HISTORICAL BACKGROUND

Prehistory of Central North Africa: Early inhabitants of the central Maghrib (also seen as Maghreb; designates North Africa west of Egypt) left behind significant remains including remnants of hominid occupation from ca. 200,000 B.C. found near Saïda. Neolithic civilization (marked by animal domestication and subsistence agriculture) developed in the Saharan and Mediterranean Maghrib between 6000 and 2000 B.C. This type of economy, so richly depicted in the Tassili-n-Ajjer cave paintings in southeastern Algeria, predominated in the Maghrib until the classical period. The amalgam of peoples of North Africa coalesced eventually into a distinct native population that came to be called Berbers. Distinguished primarily by cultural and linguistic attributes, the Berbers lacked a written language and hence tended to be overlooked or marginalized in historical accounts.

North Africa During the Classical Period: Phoenician traders arrived on the North African coast around 900 B.C. and established Carthage (in present-day Tunisia) around 800 B.C. During the classical period, Berber civilization was already at a stage in which agriculture, manufacturing, trade, and political organization supported several states. Trade links between Carthage and the Berbers in the interior grew, but territorial expansion also brought about the enslavement or military recruitment of some Berbers and the extraction of tribute from others. The Carthaginian state declined because of successive defeats by the Romans in the Punic Wars, and in 146 B.C. the city of Carthage was destroyed. As Carthaginian power waned, the influence of Berber leaders in the hinterland grew. By the second century B.C., several large but loosely administered Berber kingdoms had emerged.

Berber territory was annexed to the Roman Empire in A.D. 24. Increases in urbanization and in the area under cultivation during Roman rule caused wholesale dislocations of Berber society, and Berber opposition to the Roman presence was nearly constant. The prosperity of most towns depended on agriculture, and the region was known as the "granary of the empire." Christianity arrived in the second century. By the end of the fourth century, the settled areas had become Christianized, and some Berber tribes had converted en masse.

Islam and the Arabs: The first Arab military expeditions into the Maghrib, between 642 and 669, resulted in the spread of Islam. By 711 the Umayyads (a Muslim dynasty based in Damascus from 661 to 750), helped by Berber converts to Islam, had conquered all of North Africa. In 750 the Abbasids succeeded the Umayyads as Muslim rulers and moved the caliphate to Baghdad. Under the Abbasids, the Rustumid imamate (761–909) actually ruled most of the central Maghrib from Tahirt, southwest of Algiers. The imams gained a reputation for honesty, piety, and justice, and the court of Tahirt was noted for its support of scholarship. The Rustumid imams failed, however, to organize a reliable standing army, which opened the way for Tahirt's demise under the assault of the Fatimid dynasty. With their interest focused primarily on Egypt and Muslim lands beyond, the Fatimids left the rule of most of Algeria to the Zirids (972–1148), a Berber dynasty that centered significant local power in Algeria for the first time. This period was marked by constant conflict, political instability, and economic decline. Following a large incursion of Arab bedouins from Egypt beginning in the first half of the eleventh century, the use of Arabic spread to the countryside, and sedentary Berbers were gradually Arabized.

The Almoravid ("those who have made a religious retreat") movement developed early in the eleventh century among the Sanhaja Berbers of the western Sahara. The movement's initial impetus was religious, an attempt by a tribal leader to impose moral discipline and strict adherence to Islamic principles on followers. But the Almoravid movement shifted to engaging in military conquest after 1054. By 1106 the Almoravids had conquered Morocco, the Maghrib as far east as Algiers, and Spain up to the Ebro River.

Like the Almoravids, the Almohads ("unitarians") found their inspiration in Islamic reform. The Almohads took control of Morocco by 1146, captured Algiers around 1151, and by 1160 had completed the conquest of the central Maghrib. The zenith of Almohad power occurred between

1163 and 1199. For the first time, the Maghrib was united under a local regime, but the continuing wars in Spain overtaxed the resources of the Almohads, and in the Maghrib their position was compromised by factional strife and a renewal of tribal warfare. In the central Maghrib, the Zayanids founded a dynasty at Tlemcen in Algeria. For more than 300 years, until the region came under Ottoman suzerainty in the sixteenth century, the Zayanids kept a tenuous hold in the central Maghrib. Many coastal cities asserted their autonomy as municipal republics governed by merchant oligarchies, tribal chieftains from the surrounding countryside, or the privateers who operated out of their ports. Nonetheless, Tlemcen, the "pearl of the Maghrib," prospered as a commercial center.

The final triumph of the 700-year Christian reconquest of Spain was marked by the fall of Granada in 1492. Christian Spain imposed its influence on the Maghrib coast by constructing fortified outposts and collecting tribute. But Spain never sought to extend its North African conquests much beyond a few modest enclaves.

Privateering was an age-old practice in the Mediterranean, and North African rulers engaged in it increasingly in the late sixteenth and early seventeenth centuries because it was so lucrative. Algeria became the privateering city-state par excellence, and two privateer brothers were instrumental in extending Ottoman influence in Algeria. At about the time Spain was establishing its presidios in the Maghrib, the Muslim privateer brothers Aruj and Khair ad Din— the latter known to Europeans as Barbarossa, or Red Beard—were operating successfully off Tunisia. In 1516 Aruj moved his base of operations to Algiers but was killed in 1518. Khair ad Din succeeded him as military commander of Algiers, and the Ottoman sultan gave him the title of *beylerbey* (provincial governor). Under Khair ad Din's regency, Algiers became the center of Ottoman authority in the Maghrib. Subsequently, with the institution of a regular Ottoman administration, governors with the title of *pasha* ruled. Turkish was the official language, and Arabs and Berbers were excluded from government posts. In 1671 a new leader assumed power, adopting the title of *dey*. In 1710 the dey persuaded the sultan to recognize him and his successors as regent, replacing the pasha in that role. Although Algiers remained a part of the Ottoman Empire, the Ottoman government ceased to have effective influence there.

European maritime powers paid the tribute exacted by the rulers of the privateering states of North Africa (Algiers, Tunis, Tripoli, and Morocco) to prevent attacks on their shipping. The Napoleonic wars of the early nineteenth century diverted the attention of the maritime powers from suppressing what they derogatorily called piracy. But when peace was restored to Europe in 1815, Algiers found itself at war with Spain, the Netherlands, Prussia, Denmark, Russia, and Naples. In March of that year, the U.S. Congress also authorized naval action against the so-called Barbary States.

France in Algeria: As a result of what the French considered an insult to the French consul in Algiers by the dey in 1827, France blockaded Algiers for three years. France then used the failure of the blockade as a reason for a military expedition against Algiers in 1830. By 1848 nearly all of northern Algeria was under French control, and the new government of the Second Republic declared the occupied lands an integral part of France. Three "civil territories"— Algiers, Oran, and Constantine—were organized as French *départements* (local administrative units) under a civilian government.

Colons (colonists), or, more popularly, *pieds noirs* (literally, black feet) dominated the government and controlled the bulk of Algeria's wealth. Throughout the colonial era, they continued to block or delay all attempts to implement even the most modest reforms. From 1933 to 1936, mounting social, political, and economic crises in Algeria induced the indigenous population to engage in numerous acts of political protest, but the government responded with more restrictive laws governing public order and security. Algerian Muslims rallied to the French side at the start of World War II as they had done in World War I. But the *colons* were generally sympathetic to the collaborationist Vichy regime established following France's defeat by Nazi Germany.

In March 1943, Muslim leader Ferhat Abbas presented the French administration with the Manifesto of the Algerian People, signed by 56 Algerian nationalist and international leaders. The manifesto demanded an Algerian constitution that would guarantee immediate and effective political participation and legal equality for Muslims. Instead, the French administration in 1944 instituted a reform package based on the 1936 Viollette Plan that granted full French citizenship only to certain categories of "meritorious" Algerian Muslims, who numbered about 60,000. The tensions between the Muslim and *colon* communities exploded on May 8, 1945, V–E Day. When a Muslim march was met with violence, marchers rampaged. The army and police responded by conducting a prolonged and systematic *ratissage* (literally, raking over) of suspected centers of dissidence. According to official French figures, 1,500 Muslims died as a result of these countermeasures. Other estimates vary from 6,000 to as high as 45,000 killed.

In August 1947, the French National Assembly approved the government-proposed Organic Statute of Algeria. This law called for the creation of an Algerian Assembly with one house representing Europeans and "meritorious" Muslims and the other representing the remaining 8 million or more Muslims. Muslim and *colon* deputies alike abstained or voted against the statute but for diametrically opposed reasons: the Muslims because it fell short of their expectations and the *colons* because it went too far.

War of Independence: In the early morning hours of November 1, 1954, the National Liberation Front (Front de Libération Nationale—FLN) launched attacks throughout Algeria in the opening salvo of a war of independence. An important watershed in this war was the massacre of civilians by the FLN near the town of Philippeville in August 1955. The government claimed it killed 1,273 guerrillas in retaliation; according to the FLN, 12,000 Muslims perished in an orgy of bloodletting by the armed forces and police, as well as *colon* gangs. After Philippeville, all-out war began in Algeria.

From its origins in 1954 as ragtag *maquisards* numbering in the hundreds and armed with a motley assortment of weapons, the National Liberation Army (Armée de Libération Nationale—ALN), the military wing of the FLN, had evolved by 1957 into a disciplined fighting force of nearly 40,000 that successfully applied hit-and-run guerrilla warfare tactics. By 1956 France had committed more than 400,000 troops to Algeria. In 1958–59 the French army had won military control in Algeria, but political developments had already overtaken the French army's successes. During that period in France, opposition to the conflict was growing, and international pressure was also building on France to grant Algeria independence.

When Charles De Gaulle became premier of France in June 1958, he was given carte blanche to deal with Algeria. De Gaulle appointed a committee to draft a new constitution for France's Fifth Republic, with which Algeria would be associated but of which it would not form an integral part. Muslims, including women, were registered for the first time with Europeans on a common electoral roll to participate in a referendum to be held on the new constitution in September 1958. Despite threats of reprisal by the FLN, 80 percent of the Muslim electorate turned out to vote in September, and 96 percent of them approved the constitution. In February 1959, de Gaulle was elected president of the new Fifth Republic.

Then, in a September 1959 statement, de Gaulle uttered the words "self-determination," which he envisioned as leading to majority rule in an Algeria formally associated with France. Claiming that de Gaulle had betrayed them, the *colons*, backed by units of the army, staged an insurrection in Algiers in January 1960 that won mass support in Europe. French forces defused the insurrection. However, in April 1961 important elements of the French army joined in another unsuccessful insurrection intended to seize control of Algeria as well as topple the de Gaulle regime. This coup marked the turning point in the official attitude toward the Algerian war. De Gaulle was now prepared to abandon the *colons,* the group that no previous French government could have written off.

Talks with the FLN reopened at Evian in May 1961. In their final form, the Evian Accords allowed the *colons* equal legal protection with Algerians over a three-year period. At the end of that period, however, Europeans would be obliged to become Algerian citizens or be classified as aliens with the attendant loss of rights. The French electorate approved the Evian Accords by an overwhelming 91 percent vote in a referendum held in June 1962. On July 1, 1962, some 6 million of a total Algerian electorate of 6.5 million cast their ballots in the referendum on independence. The affirmative vote was a nearly unanimous mandate.

Independent Algeria, 1962–Present: The creation of the People's Democratic Republic of Algeria was formally proclaimed on September 25, 1962. The following day, after being named premier, Ahmed Ben Bella formed a cabinet that linked the leadership of the three power bases—the army, the party, and the government. However, Ben Bella's ambitions and authoritarian tendencies ultimately led the triumvirate to unravel and provoked increasing discontent among Algerians.

The war of national liberation and its aftermath had severely disrupted Algeria's society and economy. In addition to the physical destruction, the exodus of the *colons* deprived the country of most of its managers, civil servants, engineers, teachers, physicians, and skilled workers. The homeless and displaced numbered in the hundreds of thousands, many suffering from illness, and some 70 percent of the work force was unemployed. The months immediately following independence had witnessed the pell-mell rush of Algerians, their government, and its officials to claim the property and jobs left behind by the Europeans. In the 1963 March Decrees, Ben Bella declared that all agricultural, industrial, and commercial properties previously owned and operated by Europeans were vacant, thereby legalizing confiscation by the state.

A new constitution drawn up under close FLN supervision was approved by nationwide referendum in September 1963, and Ben Bella was confirmed as the party's choice to lead the country for a five-year term. Under the new constitution, Ben Bella as president combined the functions of chief of state and head of government with those of supreme commander of the armed forces. He formed his government with no need for legislative approval and was solely responsible for the definition and direction of its policies. Essentially, he had no effective institutional check on his powers.

Opposition leader Hosine Ait-Ahmed quit the National Assembly in 1963 to protest the increasingly dictatorial tendencies of the regime and formed a clandestine resistance movement, the Front of Socialist Forces (Front des Forces Socialistes—FFS) dedicated to overthrowing the Ben Bella regime by force. Late summer 1963 saw sporadic incidents attributed to the FFS. More serious fighting broke out a year later. The army moved quickly and in force to crush the rebellion. As minister of defense, Houari Boumediene had no qualms about sending the army to put down regional uprisings because he felt they posed a threat to the state. However, when Ben Bella attempted to co-opt allies from among some of those regionalists, tensions increased between Boumediene and Ben Bella. On June 19, 1965, Boumediene deposed Ben Bella in a military coup d'état that was both swift and bloodless.

Boumediene immediately dissolved the National Assembly and suspended the 1963 constitution. Political power resided in the Council of the Revolution, a predominantly military body intended to foster cooperation among various factions in the army and the party. Boumediene's position as head of government and head of state was not secure initially, but following attempted coups and a failed assassination attempt in 1967–68, Boumediene succeeded in consolidating power. Eleven years after he took power and after much public debate, a long-promised new constitution was promulgated in November 1976, and Boumediene was elected president with a 95 percent majority.

Boumediene's death on December 27, 1978, set off a struggle within the FLN to choose a successor. As a compromise to break a deadlock between two other candidates, Colonel Chadli Bendjedid, a moderate who had collaborated with Boumediene in deposing Ben Bella, was sworn in on February 9, 1979 (and subsequently reelected in 1984 and 1988). In June 1980, he summoned an extraordinary FLN Party Congress to produce a five-year plan to liberalize the economy and break up unwieldy state corporations. However, reform efforts failed to end high unemployment and other economic hardships, all of which fueled Islamist activism. The alienation and anger of the population were fanned by the widespread perception that the government had become corrupt and aloof. The waves of discontent crested in October 1988, when a series of strikes and walkouts by students and workers in Algiers degenerated into rioting. In response, the government declared a state of emergency and used force to quell the unrest.

The stringent measures used to put down the riots of "Black October" engendered a groundswell of outrage. In response, Benjedid conducted a house cleaning of senior officials and drew up a program of political reform. A new constitution, approved overwhelmingly in February 1989, dropped the word *socialist* from the official description of the country; guaranteed freedoms of expression, association, and meeting; but withdrew the guarantees of women's rights that had appeared in the 1976 constitution. The FLN was not mentioned in the document at all, and the army was discussed only in the context of national defense. The new laws reinvigorated politics.

Newspapers became the liveliest and freest in the Arab world, while political parties of nearly every stripe vied for members and a voice. In February 1989, the Islamic Salvation Front (Front Islamique du Salut—FIS) was founded.

Algeria's leaders were stunned in December 1991 when FIS candidates won absolute majorities in 188 of 430 electoral districts, far ahead of the FLN's 15 seats, in the first round of legislative elections. Faced with the possibility of a complete FIS takeover and under pressure from the military leadership, Benjadid dissolved parliament and then resigned in January 1992. He was succeeded by the five-member High Council of State, which canceled the second round of elections. The FIS, as well as the FLN, clamored for a return of the electoral process, but police and troops countered with massive arrests. In February 1992, violent demonstrations erupted in many cities. The government declared a one-year state of emergency and banned the FIS. The voiding of the 1991 election results led to a period of civil conflict that cost the lives of as many as 150,000 people. Periodic negotiations between the military government and Islamist rebels failed to produce a settlement.

In 1996 a referendum passed that introduced changes to the constitution enhancing presidential powers and banning Islamist parties. Presidential elections were held in April 1999. Although seven candidates qualified for election, all but Abdelaziz Bouteflika, who appeared to have the support of the military as well as the FLN, withdrew on the eve of the election amid charges of electoral fraud. Bouteflika went on to win 70 percent of the votes. Following his election to a five-year term, Bouteflika concentrated on restoring security and stability to the strife-ridden country. As part of his endeavor, he successfully campaigned to grant amnesty to thousands of members of the banned FIS. The so-called Civil Concord was approved in a nationwide referendum in September 2000. The reconciliation by no means ended all violence, but it reduced violence to manageable levels. An estimated 80 percent of those fighting the regime accepted the amnesty offer. The president also formed national commissions to study reforms of the education system, judiciary, and state bureaucracy. President Bouteflika was rewarded for his efforts at stabilizing the country when he was elected to another five-year term in April 2004, in an election contested by six candidates without military interference. In September 2005, another referendum—this one to consider a proposed Charter for Peace and National Reconciliation—passed by an overwhelming margin. The charter coupled another amnesty offer to all but the most violent participants in the Islamist uprising with an implicit pardon for security forces accused of abuses in fighting the rebels.

GEOGRAPHY

Location: Algeria is located in northwestern Africa, bordering the Mediterranean Sea between Morocco and Tunisia.

Size: Algeria has an area of almost 2.4 million square kilometers, more than four-fifths of which is desert. Nearly 3.5 times the size of Texas, Algeria is the tenth largest country in the world and the second largest in Africa.

Click to Enlarge Image

Land Boundaries: Algeria shares borders with Morocco (1,559 kilometers), Mali (1,376 kilometers), Libya (982 kilometers), Tunisia (965 kilometers), Niger (956 kilometers), Mauritania (463 kilometers), and Western Sahara (42 kilometers).

Disputed Territory: Algeria has border disputes with Morocco and Libya. Disagreements between Algeria and Morocco concern smuggling activities along the border, jurisdiction over territory in southeastern Morocco, and Morocco's claim to Western Sahara. Libya claims 32,000 square kilometers of southeastern Algeria.

Length of Coastline: Algeria's 998-kilometer northern border stretches along the southern edge of the Mediterranean Sea from Morocco in the west to Tunisia in the east.

Maritime Claims: Algeria claims a territorial sea of 12 nautical miles and an exclusive fishing zone of 32–52 nautical miles.

Topography: A sharp contrast exists between the relatively fertile, mountainous, topographically fragmented north, dominated by parallel ranges of the Atlas Mountains, and the vast expanse of the Sahara Desert in the south. The fertile Tell region in the north, extending eastward from the Moroccan border, is the country's heartland, containing most of its cities and population. The Tell is made up of the hills and plains of the narrow coastal region, several Tell Atlas mountain ranges, and intermediate valleys and basins. South of the Tell, the High Plateaus region stretches more than 600 kilometers eastward from the Moroccan border. This region consists of undulating, steppe-like plains lying between the Tell Atlas Mountains to the north and the Saharan Atlas mountains to the south. The High Plateaus region averages between 1,100 and 1,300 meters in elevation in the west, dropping to 400 meters in the east. Northeastern Algeria consists of a massif area extensively dissected into mountains, plains, and basins. It differs from the western portion of the country in that its prominent topographic features do not parallel the coast. The Algerian portion of the Sahara extends south of the Saharan Atlas for 1,500 kilometers to the borders with Niger and Mali. The desert is an otherworldly place, scarcely considered an integral part of the country. Far from being covered wholly by sweeps of sand, it is a region of great diversity. Immense areas of sand dunes occupy about one-quarter of the territory. Much of the remainder of the desert is covered by rocky platforms, and almost the entire southeastern quarter is taken up by highlands.

Principal Rivers: Algeria's largest river, the Chelif, flows 725 kilometers from the Tell Atlas into the Mediterranean Sea.

Climate: The coastal lowlands and mountain valleys are characterized by a Mediterranean climate, mild winters, and moderate rainfall. In this densely populated region, temperatures average between 21° C and 24° C in the summer and drop to 10° C to 12° C in the winter. Average temperatures and precipitation are lower in the intermountain High Plateaus region. The desert is hot and arid. Most of the country experiences little seasonal change but considerable diurnal variation in temperature. Rainfall is fairly abundant along the coastal part of the Tell, ranging from 400 to 670 millimeters annually, with the amount of precipitation increasing from west to east. Precipitation is heaviest in the northern part of eastern Algeria, where it reaches as much as 1,000 millimeters in some years. Farther inland the rainfall is less plentiful.

Natural Resources: Algeria's natural resources consist of petroleum, natural gas, iron ore, phosphates, uranium, lead, and zinc. Algeria has proven oil reserves of 12.3 billion barrels, a relatively modest amount. Proven natural gas reserves are estimated at 161.7 trillion cubic feet, the eighth largest in the world.

Land Use: In 2007 Algeria's land use was as follows: 3 percent, arable; 0 percent, permanent crops; 13 percent, permanent pastures; and 84 percent, other. More than four-fifths of Algeria's territory is desert.

Environmental Factors: A disturbing environmental trend is the encroachment of the Sahara Desert on the fertile coastal and highland Tell and inland Saharan Atlas regions. Poor farming practices and overgrazing have led to soil erosion. The dumping of sewage and waste from the petrochemical industry has damaged the Mediterranean coast. Water is scarce, so a premium is placed on conservation and desalination. For centuries desert nomads have relied on creative irrigation techniques, including the use of underground water tunnels and palm fronds to draw moisture. In 2007 General Electric was helping to build Africa's largest seawater desalination plant in Hamma, Algeria. The goal for the Hamma facility is to supply 20 percent of the water needed by the city of Algiers.

Time Zone: Algeria's time zone is Central European Time (Greenwich Mean Time plus 1 hour).

SOCIETY

Population: As of July 2007, Algeria's population was estimated to total 33.3 million. The population was growing at an annual rate of 1.2 percent. More than 90 percent of the country's population is concentrated along the Mediterranean coast, which constitutes only 12 percent of the country's land area. Therefore, the overall population density of 14.2 people per square kilometer is deceptive. About 59 percent of Algeria's population is urban. Drought conditions have led to an internal migration of farmers and herdsmen to the cities to seek other employment. High unemployment encourages emigration. In 2007 Algeria's net migration rate was estimated at −0.33 migrants per 1,000 people. Algeria also hosts more than 100,000 Sahrawi refugees from Western Sahara, who began taking refuge in Algeria in the 1970s following Spain's withdrawal and the eruption of a struggle for control of the territory. Most live in desert areas of western Algeria and depend on the United Nations and other relief agencies for their survival.

Demography: In 2007 population distribution by age was as follows: 0–14 years, 27.2 percent; 15–64 years, 67.9 percent; and 65 years and older, 4.8 percent. As this distribution indicates, Algeria has a very young population, which poses a challenge for the labor market and the education system. According to the World Health Organization, life expectancy in 2005 was 71 years (70 years for men and 72 years for women). In 2007 the birthrate was estimated at 17.11 per 1,000 people, and the death rate was estimated at 4.62 per 1,000 people. The infant mortality rate was 28.78 per 1,000 live births, and the fertility rate was 1.86 children born per woman.

Ethnic Group(s): An estimated 99 percent of the population is Arab–Berber, combining Islamic faith with North African Berber cultural identification. Europeans constitute the remaining 1 percent. Unrest persists in the Kabylie region in the northeast in response to restrictions on Berber ethnic, cultural, and linguistic rights.

Languages: The official language is Arabic. French is the language of business, and Berber (Tamazight) is also spoken. In October 2001, the government recognized Berber as a national language but not as an official language. As a result, the language issue remains contentious.

Religion: Sunni Islam is the state religion, and Muslims constitute 99 percent of the population. The remaining 1 percent of the population is Christian, mostly Roman Catholic but also Methodist and Evangelical Christian. Algeria's Jewish population is barely a trace of its former presence, reportedly numbering only about 60 persons. The government imposes restrictions on religious freedom (not all of which are strictly enforced in practice), including prohibition of proselytizing by non-Muslims, controls on imported religious materials (both Muslim and non-Muslim), and limits on public assembly by non-Muslims without a license. The government provides financial support for mosques, imams, and the study of Islam in public schools. As part of its regulation of the practice of Islam, the government prohibits the dissemination of Muslim literature promoting violence and monitors teaching in religious schools and preaching by imams in order to prevent extremism.

Education and Literacy: Algeria's literacy rate is estimated at 69–70 percent, higher than in Morocco and Egypt but subpar by international standards. The breakdown by gender is 79 percent for males and 61 percent for females. A lag persists for women despite progress since independence in 1962. Education consumes one-quarter of the national budget. Algeria faces a shortage of teachers as a result of the doubling in the number of eligible children and young adults in the last 12 years. Education is free and officially compulsory for Algerians up to age 16, but actual enrollment falls far short of 100 percent. Enrollment drops off sharply from primary to secondary school. In fact, only about half the eligible population is enrolled in secondary school, which consists of two three-year cycles beginning at age 12. In addition, Algeria has 10 universities, seven university centers (*centres universitaires*), and several technical colleges. The primary language of school instruction is Arabic, but Berber-language instruction has been permitted since 2003, in part to ease reliance on foreign teachers but also in response to complaints about Arabization.

Health: According to the latest available statistics from the World Health Organization, in 2002 Algeria had inadequate numbers of physicians (1.13 per 1,000 people), nurses (2.23 per 1,000 people), and dentists (0.31 per 1,000 people). Access to "improved water sources" was limited to 92 percent of the population in urban areas and 80 percent of the population in rural areas. Some 99 percent of Algerians living in urban areas, but only 82 percent of those living in rural areas, had access to "improved sanitation." According to the World Bank, Algeria is making progress toward its goal of "reducing by half the number of people without sustainable access to improved drinking water and basic sanitation by 2015." Given Algeria's young population, policy favors preventive health care and clinics over hospitals. In keeping with this policy, the government maintains an immunization program. However, poor sanitation and unclean water still cause tuberculosis, hepatitis, measles, typhoid fever, cholera, and dysentery. In 2003 about 0.10 percent of the population aged 15–49 was living with human immunodeficiency virus/acquired immune deficiency syndrome (HIV/AIDS). The poor generally receive health care free of charge, but the wealthy pay for care according to a sliding scale. Access to health care is enhanced by the requirement that doctors and dentists work in public health for at least five years. However, doctors are more easily found in the cities of the north than in the Sahara region in the south.

Welfare: In 2005 Algeria ranked 104 out of 177 countries in the United Nations' human development index, a measure of overall well-being. Approximately half the Algerian population lives below the poverty line. About 45 percent of wealth is concentrated in the hands of the top 5 percent of the population, a phenomenon that is partly the result of collusion among businessmen, public officials, and military officers.

ECONOMY

Overview: Algeria's economy is in the midst of a difficult and halting transition from state control to an open market. The economy depends heavily on the hydrocarbons industry, which is highly cyclical. In the current high-price environment for oil and natural gas, Algeria's economy is experiencing an upswing, and hydrocarbons account for about 60 percent of revenues, 30 percent of gross domestic product (GDP), and 95 percent of exports. However, the International Monetary Fund (IMF) is encouraging Algeria to diversify its economy, in part to reduce the country's high rate of unemployment (15.7 percent in 2006) but also to promote stability and to assist in the transition to a market economy. Under the leadership of President Abdelaziz Bouteflika (1999–), the government is pursuing an economic reform program that embraces not just diversification but also other IMF initiatives such as deregulation, banking reform, and trade liberalization. However, the program is expected to encounter bureaucratic resistance, particularly in the area of privatization. Much improvement is needed; in a 2007 survey of business conditions in 178 countries, the World Bank ranked Algeria 125 for ease of doing business.

Gross Domestic Product (GDP): In 2007 Algeria's estimated GDP was US$125.9 billion according to the official exchange rate. Using purchasing power parity, estimated GDP was US$268.9 billion, or US$8,100 on a per capita basis. The estimated real growth rate was 4.6 percent. In 2007 industry accounted for 61 percent of GDP, services constituted 31 percent, and agriculture provided the remaining 8 percent.

Government Budget: In 2007 government revenues of US$58.5 billion exceeded expenditures of US$41.4 billion. Receipts from the hydrocarbons industry usually account for roughly 60 percent of revenues.

Inflation: In 2007 the estimated inflation rate was 4.6 percent.

Agriculture, Forestry, and Fishing: Algeria's agricultural sector, which contributes about 8 percent of gross domestic product (GDP) but employs 14 percent of the workforce, is unable to meet the food needs of the country's population. As a result, some 45 percent of food is imported. The primary crops are wheat, barley, and potatoes. Farmers also have had success growing dates for export. Cultivation is concentrated in the fertile coastal plain of the Tell region, which represents just a slice of Algeria's total territory. Altogether, only about 3 percent of Algerian territory is arable. Even in the Tell, rainfall variability has a significant impact on production. Government efforts to stimulate farming in the less arable steppe and desert regions have met with limited success. However, herdsmen maintain livestock, specifically goats, cattle, and sheep, in the High Plateaus region.

Algeria's climate and periodic fires are not conducive to a thriving forestry industry. However, Algeria is a producer of cork and Aleppo pine. In 2005 roundwood removals totaled 7.8 million cubic meters, while sawnwood production amounted to only 13 million cubic meters per year.

Algeria's fishing industry does not take full advantage of the Mediterranean coast, in part because fishing is generally done from small family-owned boats instead of large commercial fishing trawlers. However, the government is attempting to boost the relatively small catch—slightly more than 125,000 metric tons in 2005—by modernizing fishing ports, permitting foreigners to fish in Algerian waters, and subsidizing fishing-related projects.

Mining and Minerals: Algeria's Ministry of Energy and Mines is responsible for overseeing the nation's mineral production. State-owned steel and gold production companies were privatized in 2001–2. In 2005 the major products of Algeria's non-energy mining sector were as follows: iron ore (151,775 gross weight metric tons); zinc concentrates (4,463 metric tons); mercury (276 kilograms); phosphate rock (878 metric tons); barite (53 metric tons); unrefined salt (197 metric tons); and crude gypsum (1,460 metric tons).

Industry and Manufacturing: In 2007 industry accounted for 61 percent of gross domestic product (GDP), but about half of that amount was attributable to the hydrocarbons sector. By contrast, manufacturing's share of GDP was only about 5 percent, and the trend line was downward. The main drag on manufacturing is inefficient state-owned enterprises, which suffer from a lack of investment and operate well below capacity. Some of Algeria's top manufactured products are cement, footwear, pig iron, steel ingots, and trucks.

Energy: A member of the Organization of the Petroleum Exporting Countries, Algeria exports both crude oil and natural gas, and elevated energy prices in recent years have led to an improvement in the country's budget, external debt, and foreign currency reserves. Algeria has proven oil reserves, as of January 2007, of 12.3 billion barrels, a relatively modest amount. Out of more than 2.1 million barrels of oil produced per day in 2006, more than 1.8 million barrels were exported. Proven natural gas reserves are estimated at 161.7 trillion cubic feet, the eighth largest in the world. Out of 2.8 trillion cubic feet of natural gas produced in 2004, 2.1 trillion cubic feet were exported. Algeria's top natural gas customers, in order, are France, Spain, Turkey, the United States, and Belgium. Algeria's largest oil field, Hassi Messaoud in the Sahara Desert, contributed 440,000 barrels per day in 2006. A hydrocarbons law passed in April 2005 removes many restrictions on foreign energy companies. In 2004 Algeria's electricity production was 29.4 billion kilowatt-hours, slightly exceeding electricity consumption of 27.4 billion kilowatt-hours.

Services: In 2007 Algeria's services sector accounted for 31 percent of gross domestic product (GDP) but employed the majority of the workforce. The services sector is undergoing deregulation and is being opened to private and foreign competition. Insurance, banking, air transportation, and air courier services already have been deregulated. However, most banks are still public, and the capital markets are severely underdeveloped. Tourism is weak, reflecting the low quality of accommodations and the fear of insurgency-related terrorism.

Banking and Finance: Algeria's banking sector is dominated by public banks, which suffer from high levels of non-performing loans to state-owned enterprises (SOEs). As of 2007, public banks controlled 95 percent of total bank assets. In 2007 nonperforming loans represented a towering 38 percent of total loans at public banks, according to International Monetary Fund (IMF) estimates. Modest progress has been made in implementing several reforms proposed by the IMF, including replacing bank credits to SOEs with government subsidies; boosting bank supervision, accountability, and transparency; and modernizing the payments system. One specific reform that has been achieved is the establishment in 2006 of the Algerian Real Time Settlements system, which facilitates the prompt and reliable electronic transfer of payments. In November 2007, the proposed sale and privatization of Crédit Populaire d'Algérie was postponed because of turbulent market conditions. Recently, HSBC and Deutsche Bank announced that they would commence commercial banking (in the case of HSBC) and investment banking (in the case of Deutsche Bank) in Algeria. Only a few companies are listed on the underdeveloped and relatively opaque Algiers stock exchange.

Tourism: Algeria's tourism industry, which contributes only about 1 percent of GDP, lags behind that of its neighbors Morocco and Tunisia. Algeria receives only about 200,000 tourists and visitors annually. Ethnic Algerian French citizens represent the largest group of tourists, followed by Tunisians. The modest level of tourism is attributable to a combination of poor hotel accommodations and the threat of terrorism. However, the government has adopted a plan known as "Horizon 2025," which is designed to address the lack of infrastructure. Various hotel operators are planning to build hotels, particularly along the Mediterranean coast. Another potential opportunity involves adventure holidays in the south. The Algerian government has set the goal of boosting the number of foreign visitors, including tourists, to 1.2 million by 2010.

Labor: The largest employer is government, which claims 32 percent of the workforce. Even though industry is a much larger part of the economy than agriculture, agriculture employs slightly more people (14 percent of the workforce) than industry (13.4 percent of the workforce). One of the reasons for this disparity is that the energy sector is very capital-intensive. Trade accounts for 14.6 percent of the workforce, while the construction and public works sector employs 10 percent, reflecting the government's efforts to upgrade the country's infrastructure and stock of affordable housing.

At the end of 2006, the unemployment rate was about 15.7 percent, but the rate among those under the age of 25 was 70 percent. In 2005 the labor participation rate was only 52 percent, versus an Organisation for Economic Co-operation and Development average of 70 percent. New entrants to the workforce and the lack of emigration options make unemployment a chronic problem and an important challenge to the government. Given its highly capital-intensive nature, the hydrocarbons industry is not in a position to employ many job seekers.

Foreign Economic Relations: In its foreign economic relations, Algeria is seeking more trade and foreign investment. For example, Algeria's hydrocarbons law passed in April 2005 is designed to encourage foreign investment in energy exploration. Increased production could raise Algeria's profile as a member of the Organization of the Petroleum Exporting Countries. In keeping with its pro-trade agenda, Algeria achieved association status with the European Union (EU) in September 2005. Over a 12-year period, the association agreement is expected to enable Algeria to export goods to the EU tariff-free, while it gradually lifts tariffs on imports from the EU. Algeria has signed bilateral investment agreements with 20 different nations, including many European countries, China, Egypt, Malaysia, and Yemen. In July 2001, the United States and Algeria agreed on a framework for discussions leading to such an agreement, but a final treaty has not yet been negotiated. Ultimately, trade liberalization, customs modernization, deregulation, and banking reform are designed to improve the country's negotiating position as it seeks accession to the World Trade Organization.

Imports: In 2007 Algerian imports totaled US$26.08 billion. The principal imports were capital goods, foodstuffs, and consumer goods. The top import partners were France (22 percent), Italy (8.6 percent), China (8.5 percent), Germany (5.9 percent), Spain (5.9 percent), the United States (4.8 percent), and Turkey (4.5 percent).

Exports: In 2007 Algeria exported US$63.3 billion, more than twice as much as it imported. Exports accounted for 30 percent of gross domestic product (GDP). Hydrocarbon products constituted at least 95 percent of export earnings. The principal exports were petroleum, natural gas, and petroleum products. The top export partners were the United States (27.2 percent), Italy (17 percent), Spain (9.7 percent), France (8.8 percent), Canada (8.1 percent), and Belgium (4.3 percent). Algeria supplies 25 percent of the European Union's natural gas imports.

Trade Balance: In 2007 Algeria posted a positive merchandise trade balance of US$37.2 billion.

Balance of Payments: In 2007 Algeria achieved a positive current account balance of US$31.5 billion. High prices for Algeria's energy exports are the main driver for the improvement in the current account balance.

External Debt: Reflecting strong oil export revenues, external debt is on a downward trajectory. For example, these revenues facilitated early repayments of US$900 million in loans from the African Development Bank and Saudi Arabia. In March 2006, Algeria's purchase of 78 aircraft from Russia led to the cancellation of Algeria's entire debt to Russia. In 2006 external debt was estimated at US$4.4 billion, down from US$23.5 billion in 2003.

Foreign Investment: In 2006 foreign direct investment (FDI) in Algeria totaled US$1.8 billion. The petrochemical, transport, and utilities sectors have been recent beneficiaries of FDI. FDI into the oil sector was expected to rise as a result of a hydrocarbons law, approved in April 2005, that created a more even playing field for foreign oil companies to compete with Algeria's state-owned oil company, Sonatrach, for exploration and production contracts. Algeria also is seeking foreign investment in power and water systems.

Foreign Aid: As of August 2006, cumulative World Bank assistance to Algeria totaled US$5.9 billion, encompassing 72 projects. Currently, the World Bank is pursuing seven projects, specifically budget modernization, mortgage finance, natural disaster recovery, energy and mining, rural employment, telecommunications, and transportation. In 2005 economic assistance to Algeria from the United States amounted to US$4.4 million, most of which was attributable to the Middle East Partnership Initiative (MEPI) and the remainder to International Military Education and Training (IMET). MEPI encourages economic, political, and educational reform in the Middle East. In 2006 IMET, which provides U.S. military training to foreign troops, had a budget of US$823 million. In 2005 the European Union contributed US$58 million to Algeria's economic development under the Euro-Mediterranean Partnership.

Currency and Exchange Rate: Algeria's currency is the dinar (DZD). The dinar is loosely linked to the U.S. dollar in a managed float. Algeria's main export, crude oil, is priced in dollars, while most of Algeria's imports are priced in euros. Therefore, the government endeavors to manage fluctuations in the value of the dinar. As of April 2008, US$1 was equivalent to about DZD64.6.

Algeria's foreign currency reserves have grown rapidly since 2000, reflecting rising prices for exported oil. At the end of 2007, foreign reserves totaled US$99.3 billion, up from US$12 billion in 2000 and the equivalent of almost four years of imports.

Fiscal Year: Calendar year.

TRANSPORTATION AND TELECOMMUNICATIONS

Overview: Since independence in 1962, Algeria's transportation system has been neglected. The country has a very limited road system and an antiquated rail network that is oriented more toward cargo than passenger traffic. Port activity revolves around the export of hydrocarbons. In the view of the World Bank, Algeria's air travel, railroad, and bus systems are too dependent on government subsidies, in contrast to the country's ports and airports, which operate self-sufficiently. A state-owned airline faces diminished private competition. Algeria's telecommunications system is also underdeveloped, particularly in rural areas.

Roads: Algeria has 107,000 kilometers of roads, 72 percent of which are paved. Road conditions are poor as a result of a lack of maintenance. An east–west expressway is planned, with most construction expected to be completed by 2010.

Railroads: Algerian National Railways (Société Nationale des Transports Ferroviaires—SNTF) manages Algeria's 4,940-kilometer rail network, which suffers from mostly antiquated rolling stock, poor signaling equipment, and low worker productivity. In 2001 SNTF purchased 15 new locomotives from General Motors. At most 300 kilometers of broad-gauge track, dedicated to cargo traffic between iron-ore mines and the port of Annaba, are electrified. Rail lines service Algiers, major cities along the Mediterranean coast, and the border with Tunisia. Terrorism against the rail system led to a decline in the number of passengers carried, the distance traveled by passengers, and the amount of freight carried during the late 1990s. In Algiers a 26.5-

kilometer metro line has been under construction since 1991 and is scheduled to open beginning in 2008.

Ports: Algeria has the following Mediterranean ports: Algiers, Annaba, Arzew, Bejaïa, Dellys, Ghazaouet, Jijel, Mostaganem, Mers el Kebir, Oran, and Skikda. The busiest port by far is Arzew, which handles about 40 percent of Algerian crude oil exports; Skikda has the second largest share. Algeria plans to expand the petrochemical facilities at Arzew, but in general the port sector suffers from a lack of investment in container handling and other equipment.

Inland Waterways: Algeria has no navigable inland waterways.

Civil Aviation and Airports: Algeria has 137 airports, 53 of which have permanent surfaces. The country's principal international airport is Algiers Houari Boumediene Airport. In 2006 the airport opened a new terminal for international operations with an annual capacity of 6 million passengers. Algeria's primary airline is state-owned Air Algérie, which dominates the sector in spite of competition from eight private airlines, notably including Khalifa Airways, which has a history of financial difficulties.

Pipelines: The state-owned Algerian oil company, Sonatrach, manages more than 2,400 kilometers of crude oil pipelines. The longest pipeline carries oil 805 kilometers from the Hassi Messaoud oil field to the port of Arzew. Sonatrach is building a parallel pipeline to more than double capacity. The only oil pipeline that crosses into another country runs 257 kilometers from the In Amenas oil field to the Tunisian export terminal at La Skhira. A network of natural gas pipelines emanates from the Hassi R'Mel natural gas field. Two pipelines carry natural gas from Algeria to Europe: the 1,078-kilometer Trans-Mediterranean Pipeline to Italy and the 1,609-kilometer Maghreb–Europe Gas Pipeline to Spain. Additional natural gas pipelines to Europe are planned. These additions should expand Algeria's gas export capacity to Italy from 30 billion cubic meters in 2005 to 88 billion cubic meters in 2010; gas export capacity to Spain is expected to grow from 12 billion cubic meters to 40 billion cubic meters over the same interval. Furthermore, Algeria and Nigeria have proposed the construction of a 4,300-kilometer trans-Saharan natural gas pipeline from Nigeria via Algeria and under the Mediterranean Sea to Europe, with a target date of 2015.

Telecommunications: Outside of the urban north, Algeria's telecommunications network is underdeveloped, and in general ownership of telephones, computers, televisions, and radios is very limited. According to the World Bank, it takes an average of 174 days to secure a telephone line in Algeria, the second longest time among 51 developing countries surveyed. However, the telecommunications sector has begun to expand since the government authorized the privatization of the sector in 2000. In accordance with this policy, Algérie Télécom, a new joint-stock company, assumed control of fixed-line and mobile telephone service from the Ministry of Posts and Telecommunications, which will be responsible for regulating the sector.

In 2005 Algeria had an average of 78 telephone mainlines and 416 mobile subscribers per 1,000 people. Telephone service is better in the north, particularly in urban areas, than in the rural south, where it is sparse. In 2005 some 88 percent of Algerian households had television sets. In 1999 there were 46 television broadcast stations, plus 216 repeaters, as well as 25 AM, one FM, and eight shortwave radio stations. In December 2007, commercial operators announced their intention to launch satellite broadcasting of three television channels and four radio stations in 2008. In 2005 Algeria had 11 personal computers and 58 Internet users per 1,000 people, respectively. In 2007 the country had 2,077 Internet hosts. In 2005 an Algerian Internet service provider began to manufacture laptop computers, setting the production goal of 1 million per year.

GOVERNMENT AND POLITICS

Government Overview: The Algerian government is a multi-party republic with a constitution and a strong presidency. In 1992 Algeria's military-led government canceled the second round of national legislative elections following the overwhelming success of an Islamist party in the first round. This action led to a popular revolt that ultimately cost the lives of as many as 150,000 people. In the early 2000s, the government offered amnesty to the rebels; violence has since abated, but a state of emergency continues. The overwhelming re-election of President Abdelaziz Bouteflika in April 2004 reflects his success in restoring relative stability to the country following a period of bloody civil strife.

Branches of Government: Algeria observes a separation of powers among the executive, legislative, and judicial branches of government. The president is the head of state and has wide-ranging powers, including the ability to appoint and dismiss the prime minister, who serves as head of government. The president is also commander in chief of the armed forces, and the current president also serves as minister of national defense. The president is elected to a five-year term and may be re-elected once. President Abdelaziz Bouteflika was elected to a second term in April 2004, reportedly with 85 percent of the vote. However, he is seeking changes to the constitution that would enable him to serve a third term beginning in 2009. Although the prime minister appoints the Council of Ministers, the president heads both the Council of Ministers and the High Security Council, which advises the president on national security issues.

Algeria has a bicameral parliament. The lower chamber is the 389-member National People's Assembly (Assemblée Populaire Nationale—APN), and the upper chamber is the 144-member Council of the Nation. Members of the APN are popularly elected for five-year terms. The last elections for the APN were held in May 2007. Regional and local authorities elect two-thirds of the Council of the Nation, while the president appoints the remaining members. The members serve six-year terms; half stand for election or appointment every three years. The Council of the Nation was last constituted according to this procedure in 2003. Legislation may originate with either of the chambers or with the president.

Although Algeria's constitution mandates an independent judiciary, the executive branch exercises some influence over its operations. Ordinary courts have initial jurisdiction over civil proceedings. Each of the 48 provinces has a court of appeal that reviews initial court decisions. The Supreme Court has the highest jurisdiction. Administrative courts have jurisdiction over minor disputes. The State Council, which was established in 1998, regulates the administrative courts. The Court of Auditors oversees public spending and services. The nine-member Constitutional Council ensures that legislation is consistent with the constitution and supervises elections. The High Islamic Council encourages the application of Islamic case law. Military courts have jurisdiction over cases involving security- or terrorism-related charges brought against both military personnel and civilians.

Constitution: Algeria's constitution was adopted on November 19, 1976. It was subsequently modified in 1979 and amended in 1988, 1989, and 1996. The constitution mandates a multi-party state, but the Ministry of Interior must approve all parties. Article 2 designates Islam as the state religion.

Administrative Divisions: Algeria is divided into 48 provinces (*wilayas*; sing., *wilaya*): Adrar, Aïn Defla, Aïn Temouchent, Alger, Annaba, Batna, Bechar, Bejaïa, Biskra, Blida, Bordj Bou Arreridj, Bouira, Boumerdes, Chelif, Constantine, Djelfa, El Bayadh, El Oued, El Tarf, Ghardaïa, Guelma, Illizi, Jijel, Khenchela, Laghouat, Mascara, Médéa, Mila, Mostaganem, M'Sila, Naama, Oran, Ouargla, Oum el Bouaghi, Relizane, Saïda, Sétif, Sidi Bel Abbes, Skikda, Souk Ahras, Tamanghasset, Tébessa, Tiaret, Tindouf, Tipaza, Tissemsilt, Tizi Ouzou, and Tlemcen. Provinces are further subdivided into communes.

Provincial and Local Government: A governor (*wali*), appointed by the president and subordinate to the Ministry of Interior, heads each of Algeria's 48 provinces. Elected assemblies govern each province and commune, the next lower administrative division. In November 2005, the government held special regional elections to address under-representation of Berber interests in regional and local assemblies.

Judicial and Legal System: The top three sources of Algerian law are treaties or conventions ratified by the president, the legal code, and Islamic law. French jurisprudence has not been observed since 1975. According to the constitution, defendants are entitled to a public trial, during which they are presumed innocent, they may confront witnesses, and they may present evidence. They also have the right to appeal the verdict. Despite these constitutional protections, defendants, particularly women, are sometimes denied due process, including the opportunity to examine government evidence, according to the U.S. Department of State.

Electoral System: Universal suffrage applies at age 18. Presidential elections, which are held every five years, are next scheduled for April 2009. Legislative elections, also held every five years, were held on schedule in May 2007. Three parties allied with President Bouteflika won a total of 249 out of 389 seats in the National People's Assembly.

Politics and Political Parties: The Ministry of Interior must approve all political parties, and, according to the constitution, membership may not be "based on differences in religion, language, race, gender, or region." The most influential political party is the National Liberation Front (Front de Libération Nationale—FLN), which holds 136 out of 389 seats in the National People's Assembly. President Abdelaziz Bouteflika does not officially belong to any political party, but he is honorary chairman of the FLN. In February 2005, the FLN voted to support Bouteflika after a dissident faction agreed to drop opposition to his policies. Other major parties are the Front of Socialist Forces, the Movement for National Reform, the Movement of Society for Peace, and the National Rally for Democracy. In 1992 the government outlawed the Islamic Salvation Front. Altogether, Algeria has about 40 political parties.

Mass Media: Algeria has more than 45 independent French-language and Arabic-language publications as well as four government-owned newspapers (two published in French and two in Arabic), but the government controls all printing presses and advertising. The newspapers with the largest circulations are *El-Khabar* (530,000), *Quotidien d'Oran* (195,000), and *Liberté* (120,000); all three are employee-owned. The government also owns all radio and television outlets, which provide pro-government programming. In 2004 and 2005, the government increased the access of Berber language and culture to both print and broadcast media.

In general, the state exercises considerable control over Algeria's mass media, and harassment of the press increased following President Bouteflika's re-election in April 2004. The print media practice self-censorship to avoid various forms of government pressure, including defamation lawsuits and the potential withholding of state-controlled advertising. In 2004 two newspapers were closed or suspended over debts owed the state-owned printing company. In its 2007 *Freedom of the Press* report, Freedom House classified Algeria as "not free," reflecting the government's policy of harassing, intimidating, and sometimes imprisoning journalists. During the civil strife from 1993 to 1997, mostly Islamist factions murdered some 57 journalists.

Foreign Relations: Algeria maintains diplomatic relations with more than 100 countries. From January 2004 until December 2005, Algeria held a non-permanent, rotating seat on the United Nations Security Council. Algeria and the United States have a somewhat ambivalent relationship, but the two countries formed strategic ties in the battle against radical Islam following the September 11, 2001, terrorist attacks on the United States. Relations between Algeria and France also are ambivalent because of the mixed legacy of French colonialism. However, the French language remains influential, and France is a major trading partner for Algeria. In December 2007, Algeria and France signed a new agreement for scientific and cultural cooperation. They also agreed to cooperate in the development of nuclear energy for civilian uses. In Africa, Algeria's diplomatic initiatives include hosting peace talks between Ethiopia and Eritrea in 2000, cooperating with Egypt, Nigeria, Senegal, and South Africa on the New Partnership for Africa's Development (an African Union development initiative), and promoting the Arab Maghreb Union (an economic bloc encompassing Algeria, Libya, Mauritania, Morocco, and Tunisia). Algeria supports the Polisario, a Western Sahara independence movement, by providing it with sanctuary in southwestern Algeria. The border region between Morocco and Algeria has been the site of terrorist violence. Although Morocco lifted visa requirements for Algerians in 2004, Algeria has declined to reciprocate. In the Middle East, Algeria advocates the Palestinian cause.

Membership in International Organizations: Algeria belongs to the following international organizations: African Development Bank, African Union, Arab Bank for Economic Development in Africa, Arab Fund for Economic and Social Development, Arab Maghreb Union, Arab Monetary Fund, Bank for International Settlements, Food and Agriculture Organization, Group of 15, Group of 24, Group of 77, International Atomic Energy Agency, International Bank for Reconstruction and Development (World Bank), International Chamber of Commerce, International Civil Aviation Organization, International Confederation of Free Trade Unions, International Criminal Court (signatory), International Criminal Police Organization, International Development Association, International Federation of Red Cross and Red Crescent Societies, International Finance Corporation, International Fund for Agricultural Development,

International Hydrographic Organization, International Labour Organization, International Maritime Organization, International Monetary Fund, International Olympic Committee, International Organization for Migration, International Organization for Standardization, International Red Cross and Red Crescent Movement, International Telecommunication Union, Islamic Development Bank, League of Arab States, Multilateral Investment Geographic Agency, Nonaligned Movement, Organisation for the Prohibition of Chemical Weapons, Organization for Security and Co-operation in Europe (partner), Organization of American States (observer), Organization of Arab Petroleum Exporting Countries, Organization of the Islamic Conference, Organization of the Petroleum Exporting Countries, United Nations, United Nations Conference on Trade and Development, United Nations Educational, Scientific and Cultural Organization, United Nations High Commissioner for Refugees, United Nations Industrial Development Organization, Universal Postal Union, World Customs Organization, World Health Organization, World Intellectual Property Organization, World Meteorological Organization, World Tourism Organization, and World Trade Organization (observer).

Major International Treaties: In the area of arms control, Algeria is a party to the following conventions: Biological Weapons, Chemical Weapons, Nuclear Nonproliferation, and Partial Test Ban. Algeria has signed, but not ratified, the Nuclear Test Ban Treaty and the Geneva Protocol. Regarding the environment, Algeria is a party to the following conventions: Biodiversity, Climate Change, Desertification, Endangered Species, Environmental Modification, Law of the Sea, Ozone Layer Protection, Ship Pollution, and Wetlands. In the area of counterterrorism, Algeria is a party to the following conventions: Suppression of the Financing of Terrorism, Suppression of Terrorist Bombings, Marking of Plastic Explosives for the Purpose of Detection, Against the Taking of Hostages, Offences and Certain Other Acts Committed on Board Aircraft, Suppression of Unlawful Seizure of Aircraft, Suppression of Unlawful Acts against the Safety of Civil Aviation, Protocol on the Suppression of Unlawful Acts of Violence at Airports Serving International Civil Aviation, Suppression of Unlawful Acts against the Safety of Maritime Navigation, and Prevention and Punishment of Crimes against Internationally Protected Persons, including Diplomatic Agents.

NATIONAL SECURITY

Armed Forces Overview: Algeria's military, paramilitary, and police forces are more concerned about an internal threat from Islamic extremists than a definable external threat. The military is attempting to control the internal threat through operational and surveillance activities. Russia has supplied most of the military's equipment.

Foreign Military Relations: Algeria's leading arms supplier is Russia, and the second most important supplier is China. In March 2006, Algeria purchased 78 aircraft from Russia, leading to the cancellation of Algeria's entire debt to Russia. The United States has been reluctant to provide Algeria with arms, although the two nations began a dialogue on military relations in 2004. The United States trains Algerian troops under the International Military Education and Training (IMET) program.

External Threat: Algeria does not face a clearly defined external threat. Theoretically, Algeria could become embroiled in a serious dispute with neighboring Morocco over Algeria's support for the Polisario Front, a Western Saharan independence movement.

Defense Budget: In 2006 Algeria's defense expenditures totaled about US$3 billion, corresponding to about 3 percent of gross domestic product (GDP).

Major Military Units: Algeria's active-duty military consists of 120,000 in the army (including 75,000 conscripts), 7,500 in the navy and coast guard, and 10,000 in the air force. In addition to active-duty personnel, Algeria has about 150,000 military reserves assigned to the army. The army is organized in six military regions. Possible reorganization into a divisional structure is on hold. Major army units include two armored divisions, three mechanized divisions, one airborne division, one independent armored brigade, and five independent mechanized infantry brigades. Additional battalions are as follows: 20 independent infantry, two artillery, five air defense, and six antiaircraft artillery. The air force is organized in five fighter/ground attack squadrons, eight fighter squadrons, two reconnaissance squadrons, two maritime patrol squadrons, two transport squadrons, one tanker squadron, four attack helicopter squadrons, seven transport helicopter squadrons, and 10 training squadrons. The navy and coast guard have bases at Mers el Kebir, Algiers, Annaba, and Jijel.

Major Military Equipment: According to the most recent issue of *The Military Balance*, published annually by the International Institute for Security Studies, Algeria's army has the following equipment: 920 main battle tanks, 139 reconnaissance vehicles, 1,084 armored infantry fighting vehicles, 910 armored personnel carriers, 375 towed artillery, 170 self-propelled artillery, 144 multiple rocket launchers, 330 mortars, an unspecified number of antitank guided weapons, 180 recoilless launchers, 300 antitank guns, at least 288 surface-to-air missiles, about 875 air defense guns, and an unspecified number of surface-to-air missiles. The navy has two submarines, nine principal surface combatants, 22 patrol and coastal combatants, three amphibious craft, and three logistics and support craft. The air force has 204 combat aircraft and 33 attack helicopters.

Military Service: Military service is compulsory for males aged 19–30. The term of service is 18 months, consisting of six months of basic training and 12 months of civil projects.

Paramilitary Forces: Algeria's paramilitary forces include the 20,000-member Gendarmerie Nationale, which is subordinate to the Ministry of National Defense; the 1,200-member Republican Guard, an elite corps of the Gendarmerie Nationale; an estimated 16,000 national security forces in the General Directorate of National Security under the Ministry of Interior; and 150,000 militia and guards.

Foreign Military Forces: No foreign forces are based in Algeria.

Military Forces Abroad: Algeria has deployed observers with United Nations Missions in Burundi, the Democratic Republic of the Congo, Ethiopia and Eritrea, and Sudan.

Police: Responsibility for maintaining law and order is shared by the 60,000-member Gendarmerie Nationale, under the Ministry of National Defense, and the 30,000-member Sûreté Nationale, or national police force, under the Ministry of Interior. The Gendarmerie Nationale is mainly active in rural and remote areas of the country, while the Sûreté Nationale is primarily an urban police force. Algeria's various security forces have been involved in counterterrorism operations and have been accused of excesses in the battle against Islamist groups. They also face complaints of harassing journalists.

Internal Threat: Algeria faces a threat from domestic Islamist radical groups. In December 2007, Al-Qaeda in the Islamic Maghreb (AQIM) carried out dual suicide bomb attacks in Algiers against a Coast Guard barracks in Dellys and Algerian President Abdelaziz Bouteflika in Batna. The attacks resulted in about 52 deaths, but President Bouteflika was not harmed. Islamist groups rose up in rebellion in 1992 after the government halted a national election that would have given power to the militant Islamic Salvation Front. Related terrorism, which cost the lives of as many as 150,000 people, has abated since the government began to offer amnesty to rebels. Berber unrest also remains a concern and periodically manifests itself in the form of demonstrations to protest restrictions on ethnic, cultural, and linguistic rights.

Terrorism: Al-Qaeda in the Islamic Maghreb (AQIM) is the successor organization to the Salafist Group for Preaching and Combat (Groupe Salafiste pour la Prédication et le Combat—GSPC), one of two groups that had been competing for influence in Algeria. The other was the Armed Islamic Group (Groupe Islamique Armé—GIA). Al Qaeda was instrumental in establishing the GSPC as an alternative to the GIA, which continues to operate in a diminished form. In 1996 Osama bin Laden encouraged the GSPC to break away from the GIA because he disapproved of the GIA's extremely unpopular policy of massacring Muslim civilians who were not jihadists. Bin Laden shares the GSPC's Salafist beliefs, which advocate a restoration of the stringent form of Sunni Islam practiced by companions of the Prophet Muhammad. Although avoiding wanton violence against civilians, the GSPC targets the security services of Algeria's secular government. In one notorious incident in 2003, the GSPC seized European tourists visiting the Sahara Desert. Fourteen of the hostages were released after more than five months in exchange for ransom paid by the German government; the fifteenth hostage died while in custody.

After 1992 terrorism flared when the government canceled the second round of elections in which an Islamist party, the Islamic Salvation Front, held a substantial lead after the first round. Ensuing civil strife led to the death of as many as 150,000 people. In the early 2000s, the government offered amnesty to the rebels; violence has since abated, but a state of emergency continues. President Bouteflika, who was re-elected in April 2004, enjoys broad support because of the success of his amnesty programs in ushering in a period of relative stability. In September 2005, Bouteflika's approach was once again endorsed when a popular referendum on the Charter for Peace and National Reconciliation passed by an overwhelming margin. The charter provides for a continuing amnesty program for all but the most violent insurgents, exoneration of the security services for alleged misdeeds in fighting the insurgency, and compensation for the victims of violence.

Human Rights: In its annual country report on human rights practices released March 2008, the U.S. Department of State noted the persistence of a number of human rights problems in Algeria. Continuing problems listed in the report include failure to account for past disappearances; alleged incidences of abuse and torture of detainees; official impunity, arbitrary arrest and prolonged pretrial detention; denial of due process and fair trials; limited judicial independence; restrictions on civil liberties such as freedoms of speech, religion, press, and assembly; government corruption; and discrimination against women and minorities. According to Transparency International's Corruption Perceptions Index, Algeria ranked 99 out of 179 countries in transparency in 2007.